THE EVOLUTION
OF AFRICA'S MAJOR NATIONS

Zimbabwe

THE EVOLUTION
OF AFRICA'S MAJOR NATIONS

Zimbabwe

Michael Baughan

Mason Crest
Philadelphia

Mason Crest
370 Reed Road
Broomall, PA 19008
www.masoncrest.com

CPSIA Compliance Information: Batch #EAMN2012-26. For further information,
contact Mason Crest at 1-866-MCP-Book.

First printing

1 3 5 7 9 8 6 4 2

Library of Congress Cataloging-in-Publication Data

Baughan, Michael Gray, 1973-
Zimbabwe / Michael Baughan.
     p. cm. — (The evolution of Africa's major nations.)
Includes bibliographical references and index.
ISBN 978-1-4222-2188-4 (hardcover)
ISBN 978-1-4222-2216-4 (pbk.)
ISBN 978-1-4222-9429-1 (ebook)
1. Zimbabwe--Juvenile literature. I. Title. II. Series: Evolution of Africa's major nations.
DT2889.B3852 2011
968.91—dc22
                              2010048001

Africa: Facts and Figures
The African Union
Algeria
Angola
Botswana
Burundi
Cameroon
Democratic Republic
of the Congo

Egypt
Ethiopia
Ghana
Ivory Coast
Kenya
Liberia
Libya
Morocco
Mozambique

Nigeria
Rwanda
Senegal
Sierra Leone
South Africa
Sudan
Tanzania
Uganda
Zimbabwe

Table of Contents

Africa: Progress, Problems, and Promise

Robert I. Rotberg

Africa is the cradle of humankind, but for millennia it was off the familiar, beaten path of global commerce and discovery. Its many peoples therefore developed largely apart from the diffusion of modern knowledge and the spread of technological innovation until the 17th through 19th centuries. With the coming to Africa of the book, the wheel, the hoe, and the modern rifle and cannon, foreigners also brought the vastly destructive transatlantic slave trade, oppression, discrimination, and onerous colonial rule. Emerging from that crucible of European rule, Africans created nationalistic movements and then claimed their numerous national independences in the 1960s. The result is the world's largest continental assembly of new countries.

There are 53 members of the African Union, a regional political grouping, and 48 of those nations lie south of the Sahara. Fifteen of them, including mighty Ethiopia, are landlocked, making international trade and economic growth that much more arduous and expensive. Access to navigable rivers is limited, natural harbors are few, soils are poor and thin, several countries largely consist of miles and miles of sand, and tropical diseases have sapped the strength and productivity of innumerable millions. Being landlocked, having few resources (although countries along Africa's west coast have tapped into deep offshore petroleum and gas reservoirs), and being beset by malaria, tuberculosis, schistosomiasis, AIDS, and many other maladies has kept much of Africa poor for centuries.

Thirty-two of the world's poorest 44 countries are African. Hunger is common. So is rapid deforestation and desertification. Unemployment rates are often over 50 percent, for jobs are few—even in agriculture. Where Africa once

A Zimbabwean woman who suffers from AIDS sits on a blanket in the shade of a tree in her kraal (farm) near Katerere, Zimbabwe. The high rate of HIV/AIDS infection in Zimbabwe has contributed to the country's economic and social woes.

was a land of small villages and a few large cities, with almost everyone engaged in growing grain or root crops or grazing cattle, camels, sheep, and goats, today more than half of all the more than 1 billion Africans, especially those who live south of the Sahara, reside in towns and cities. Traditional agriculture hardly pays, and a number of countries in Africa—particularly the smaller and more fragile ones—can no longer feed themselves.

There is not one Africa, for the continent is full of contradictions and variety. Of the 750 million people living south of the Sahara, at least 150 million live in Nigeria, 85 million in Ethiopia, 68 million in the Democratic Republic of the Congo, and 49 million in South Africa. By contrast, tiny Djibouti and Equatorial Guinea have fewer than 1 million people each, and prosperous Botswana and Namibia each are under 2.2 million in population. Within some

The enormous Kariba Dam is 420 feet (128 meters) tall and 1,900 feet (579 m) long, making it one of the largest hydroelectric dams in the world. A power generating station has been supplying electricity to Zimbabwe since 1960.

countries, even medium-sized ones like Zambia (12 million), there are a plethora of distinct ethnic groups speaking separate languages. Zambia, typical with its multitude of competing entities, has 70 such peoples, roughly broken down into four language and cultural zones. Three of those languages jostle with English for primacy.

Given the kaleidoscopic quality of African culture and deep-grained poverty, it is no wonder that Africa has developed economically and politically less rapidly than other regions. Since independence from colonial rule, weak governance has also plagued Africa and contributed significantly to the widespread poverty of its peoples. Only Botswana and offshore Mauritius have been governed democratically without interruption since independence. Both are among Africa's wealthiest countries, too, thanks to the steady application of good governance.

Aside from those two nations, and South Africa, Africa has been a continent of coups since 1960, with massive and oil-rich Nigeria suffering incessant periods of harsh, corrupt, autocratic military rule. Nearly every other country on or around the continent, small and large, has been plagued by similar bouts of instability and dictatorial rule. In the 1970s and 1980s Idi Amin ruled Uganda capriciously and Jean-Bedel Bokassa proclaimed himself emperor of the Central African Republic. Macias Nguema of Equatorial Guinea was another in that same mold. More recently Daniel arap Moi held Kenya in thrall and Robert Mugabe has imposed himself on once-prosperous Zimbabwe. In both of those cases, as in the case of Gnassingbe Eyadema in Togo and the late Mobutu Sese Seko in Congo, these presidents stole wildly and drove entire peoples and their nations into penury. Corruption is common in Africa, and so are a weak rule-of-law framework, misplaced development, high expenditures on soldiers and low expenditures on health and education, and a widespread (but not universal) refusal on the part of leaders to work well for their followers and citizens.

Conflict between groups within countries has also been common in Africa. More than 12 million Africans have been killed in civil wars since 1990, while another 9 million have become refugees. Decades of conflict in Sudan led to a January 2011 referendum in which the people of southern Sudan voted overwhelmingly to secede and form a new state. In early 2011, anti-government protests spread throughout North Africa, ultimately toppling long-standing regimes in Tunisia and Egypt. That same year, there were serious ongoing hostilities within Chad, Ivory Coast, Libya, the Niger Delta region of Nigeria, and Somalia.

Despite such dangers, despotism, and decay, Africa is improving. Botswana and Mauritius, now joined by South Africa, Senegal, Kenya, and Ghana, are beacons of democratic growth and enlightened rule. Uganda and Senegal are taking the lead in combating and reducing the spread of AIDS, and others are following. There are serious signs of the kinds of progressive economic policy changes that might lead to prosperity for more of Africa's peoples. The trajectory in Africa is positive.

One of Africa's most beautiful countries, Zimbabwe is home to majestic
mountains, high plateaus, and an intri-
cate river system. (Opposite) Victoria
Falls, on Zimbabwe's western border
with Zambia, is one of the nation's
more popular attractions. (Right) A
group of Zimbabwean children in a
grassy field. Much of the country is
veld, or flat grassland.

A Tableland Set for a Feast

FOR MOST OF its history, Zimbabwe has been all too familiar with strife and conflict. However, it has rarely lacked for natural treasures, which include a temperate climate, high plateaus, and abundant natural resources.

Larger than Germany but slightly smaller than California, Zimbabwe is a landlocked country in southern Africa. To the north is Zambia; to the east/northeast is Mozambique; to the south, South Africa; and to the west, Botswana.

GEOGRAPHICAL REGIONS

Zimbabwe is most commonly divided into four geographic regions—three based on altitude and climate, and one for its contrasting terrain. Three of these regions bear the name of *veld*, a word to describe open grasslands on a high plateau. The *Afrikaners*, the Dutch people who colonized in nearby South Africa, coined the term for this feature, which dominates the Zimbabwean landscape.

The highveld contains land above 4,000 feet (1,220 meters) and comprises between one-fifth and one-quarter of the country's total area. The vast majority of the highveld is found on the Central Plateau, a tableland that runs southwest to northeast. The middleveld is made up of land situated between 1,970 and 4,000 feet (600–1,220 meters) above sea level and roughly encircles the Central Plateau. Parts of the country lying at or below 1,970 feet (600 meters) are called the lowveld. These hot and dry areas of Zimbabwe are limited to the Zambezi Valley in the north and the Sabi, Lundi, and Limpopo Basins to the southeast.

The fourth region, the Eastern Highlands that mark Zimbabwe's border with Mozambique, stand in stark contrast to the flat plateaus of the veld. This mountainous zone contains numerous peaks above 5,400 feet (1,800 meters); the highest of these peaks is Mount Inyangani, which reaches 8,504 feet (2,592 meters).

RIVER SYSTEM

Although Zimbabwe is periodically afflicted by severe droughts, the combination of a relatively high altitude and a five-month-long rainy season (November–March) makes for a large *watershed* and many rivers and streams. Generally speaking, all of Zimbabwe's major drainage systems start on the Central Plateau and flow downward, ultimately feeding one of the country's three major rivers: the Zambezi, the Limpopo, and the Sabi. All three rivers run on into Mozambique (there the Sabi is called the Save) and eventually drain into the Indian Ocean.

The largest river, the Zambezi, begins in northern Zambia and passes through Angola and back into Zambia before running along the Zambia-Zimbabwe border, where it plunges over wondrous Victoria Falls. En route it enters a deep gorge and drains into Lake Kariba, one of the largest man-made lakes in the world.

A sunset view an island in Lake Kariba, one of the world's largest artificial lakes. It is formed by Kariba Dam, which was built in 1960 to control the flow of the Zambezi River.

THE GEOGRAPHY OF ZIMBABWE

Location: Southern Africa, between South Africa and Zambia

Area: (slightly larger than Montana)
  total: 150,872 square miles (390,757 sq km)
  land: 149,362 square miles (386,847 sq km)
  water: 1,509 square miles (3,910 sq km)

Borders: Botswana, 505 miles (813 km); Mozambique, 765 miles (1,231 km); South Africa, 140 miles (225 km); Zambia, 495 miles (797 km)

Climate: tropical; moderated by altitude; rainy season (November to March)

Terrain: mostly high plateau with higher central plateau (high veldt); mountains in east

Elevation extremes:
  lowest point: junction of the Lundi and Sabi Rivers, 532 feet (162 meters)
  highest point: Inyangani, 8,504 feet (2,592 meters)

Natural hazards: recurring droughts; floods and severe storms are rare

Source: CIA World Factbook, 2011.

The next-largest river is the Limpopo, situated almost directly opposite the country from the Zambezi. This river originates in South Africa and, after entering Zimbabwe and turning due east to join the Sashe River, forms a natural border between the two countries. En route to Mozambique, the Limpopo is also fed by a number of lesser rivers flowing south/southeast.

The last of Zimbabwe's noteworthy rivers, the Sabi, flows southeast and out of the highveld, then intersects with the Lundi in the southeast corner of the country at the Mozambique border. The Sabi-Lundi basin is a hot, dry floodplain that marks the lowest point in Zimbabwe and is also home to the country's second-largest game preserve, Gonarezhou National Park. Gonarezhou has recently become part of the Great Limpopo Transfrontier

Park—or as it is commonly called, a "peace park"—jointly owned by Zimbabwe, South Africa, and Mozambique.

Although the range of this watershed is vast, it does not supply water for all of Zimbabwe's needs. Periodic droughts and an extremely dry winter season keep most of the smaller rivers and even a few of the larger ones from flowing year-round. Additionally, the country has few natural lakes. Conservation therefore plays a major role in insuring a deep water supply for agriculture to flourish, but in the worst of times even these efforts are not enough. Droughts in the years 1981–1983, 1990–1991, and 2002–2003 resulted in crop loss, severe food shortages, and the deaths of millions of cattle.

Another dry spell in 2010 wreaked havoc on Zimbabwe's already struggling farming industry. The U.S.-funded Famine Early Warning System Network (FEWSNET) estimated that as much as 18 percent of the population will have to rely on food aid until the situation improves.

The building of numerous dams and the creation of the Zimbabwe National Water Authority in 1996 have helped to lessen the impact of drought somewhat, but frequent crop failures and food shortages suggest that much more work and planning lie ahead before Zimbabwe is able to successfully manage its water supply.

A WILDLIFE PARADISE

The same conditions that have made Zimbabwe a pleasant place to live for humans since the dawn of our species have also made it an ideal animal habitat. Until modern development and the human population explosion began to adversely affect Zimbabwe's huge stretches of wilderness—or *bush*, as it is called by the locals—the country had one of the richest arrays of wildlife in the world. Comparatively speaking, it still does. Much of its flora and fauna have survived through prehistoric eras to the present day.

Zimbabwe's two main wildlife refuges are found in Hwange and Gonarezhou National Parks. With a total area of 5,614 square miles (14,540 square kilometers), Hwange is by far the larger of the two. Located in Matabeleland North Province, with the Botswana border forming its western edge, Hwange National Park is an animal-lover's paradise. In addition to countless varieties of plants, insects, and birds, over 100 species of mammals live in the park, including lions, leopards, cheetahs, and buffalo, to name only a few. Most impressive of all, 30,000 elephants are estimated to live there. However, recent poaching has eradicated many animals, and two local species, the white and black rhinos, nearly became extinct. These rhinos are making a comeback after a reintroduction to the area that began in the 1960s.

The grasslands that constitute the bulk of Hwange National Park are not quite as welcoming for trees as they are for animals. The baobab tree manages to grow there, however. This tree, which has become something of a national symbol, is a hearty *deciduous species*, and can grow 65 feet (20 meters) high and 164 feet (50 meters) around—large enough to fit 40 people inside! Baobab trees have also been known to live as long as 3,000 years. The most amazing thing about this tree is its otherworldly appearance. It has a fire-resistant, pinkish-gray bark that literally glows at sunrise and sunset, with a bulky trunk and spindly, many-forked branches that make it look like it was planted upside down.

An elephant takes a drink in Hwange National Park. The foremost refuge of Zimbabwe, this park has two dozen mammal species as well as numerous types of birds, plants, and insects.

Other trees that grow naturally in Zimbabwe's forests include African teak, mahogany, and msasa, but the demand for these hardwoods on the international market has led to rampant deforestation. Trees that have been introduced to the African habitat—pine, eucalyptus, and wattle trees—are widely grown on plantations as sources of fuel and lumber.

RICH MINERAL DEPOSITS

Zimbabwe is also endowed with a wealth of mineral deposits. Gold has been mined from as early as the Iron Age, which began before 1000 B.C. Gold trading initiated the first major contact with Zimbabwe to the outside world (beginning with the Arabs in the 8th century), and by the early part of the 20th century, gold mining was the country's most lucrative industry.

The *kopjes*, or granite outcroppings, of Matobo National Park, about 25 miles (40 km) southwest of Bulawayo, are natural treasures. The park contains most of the country's roughly 6,000 rock art sites.

In addition to gold, the country has large deposits of iron, copper, silver, gemstones (emeralds and diamonds, among others), asbestos, chrome, nickel, and coal. This natural bounty has not always been a blessing for the country, as it has been exploited by different foreign powers. Nevertheless, the management of these resources remains a prime asset in Zimbabwe's quest for a better tomorrow.

THE SMOKE THAT THUNDERS

Unique natural wonders can be found in every corner of Zimbabwe. Chief among them is Victoria Falls, the largest waterfall in the world, which lies in the extreme northwest of the country. Victoria Falls is nearly twice as high and wide as Niagara Falls, and is known to indigenous peoples as Mosi oa Tunya (the Smoke That Thunders) for a towering spray and mighty rumble that can be seen and heard from many miles away. In 1959, Kariba Dam was built to harness all that power, resulting in the creation of the massive Lake Kariba.

In the southwest lie the Matopo Hills, a region full of caves and massive boulders perched atop granite outcrops like a giant's forgotten marble collection. Hidden in these sacred hills are the ancient burial grounds of the San people, Zimbabwe's original inhabitants. There are also many rock art sites where the San painted animals and other depictions of daily life over 9,000 years ago.

Last but not least, running the entire length of the country's eastern border is a series of mountain ranges that rival any highlands in Africa for sheer scenic beauty. Stretched out beneath them are equally breathtaking valleys where coffee, tea, and various fruits are grown in Zimbabwe's most fertile fields.

Ancient rock paintings by the nomadic San people, such as this one depicting horses, can be found throughout the Matopo Hills.

The Shona, Zimbabwe's dominant ethnic group, have a long history in southern Africa. (Opposite) A traditional Shona home. (Right) Closeup of Shona stonework dating from the 11th century. The word *zimbabwe* derives from the Shona phrase *dzimba dza mabwe*, "houses of stone," which originally referred to a set of sacred buildings at Great Zimbabwe.

2 Struggle and Liberation

STONE TOOLS DATING to around 40,000 B.C. provide the earliest evidence of human habitation in Zimbabwe, but humans may have lived in this part of southern Africa much earlier. Around 7000 B.C., prehistoric Zimbabweans began to paint and carve images of wildlife and hunting scenes onto exposed granite outcroppings, or *kopjes*, and in the rock shelters where they dwelled.

Most of Zimbabwe's rock art is attributed to the San, a predominantly nomadic people who roamed the land from the Middle to Late Stone Age. Today, isolated groups of the San's descendants, commonly called "Bushmen," can still be found in southern Africa, mainly in the Kalahari Desert.

Historical records indicate that approximately 2,000 years ago, successive waves of taller, more technologically advanced peoples from northern Africa began to migrate southward and displace or intermarry with the

San. It is believed that these migrants were members of the Bantu, a large African group whose subgroups include the Shona and Ndebele, two peoples that make up the vast majority of modern-day Zimbabweans. The Bantu brought with them a sophisticated knowledge of three key technologies—pottery, farming, and the use of iron for tools and weapons. Together, these technologies signaled the coming of the Iron Age in Zimbabwe.

HOUSES OF STONE

The Shona became the dominant force in shaping the country, and still make up 82 percent of the present-day population. The ancestors of the modern-day Shona first arrived in the seventh century A.D. Through their superior organization and technological know-how, they quickly achieved a dominant position among the groups already settled there.

In addition to making their own style of pottery, the Shona also developed methods of mining gold, weaving baskets, and building with stone. In time, they built an empire that stretched from the Zambezi to the Limpopo and as far east as the Indian Ocean. The legacy of that empire lives on in the ruins of Great Zimbabwe, the historic settlement and power stronghold that gave the modern country its name. Many of the structures are still standing today. One irregularly shaped structure called the Great Enclosure has massive walls measuring 800 feet (244 meters) long, 16 feet (5 meters) thick, and 25 feet (7.5 meters) high. These dimensions make the Great Enclosure the largest stone structure in Africa south of the Egyptian Pyramids. The site likely served the purposes of citadel, palace, and religious shrine at different times throughout the years. Among other relics found there were eight finely wrought soapstone sculptures, the so-called Zimbabwe Birds whose images now adorn the country's flag and currency. These figures are thought to embody the spirits of the ancestral kings who ruled Great Zimbabwe.

At the same time the Shona built Great Zimbabwe, they also developed trade routes to the Indian Ocean. They traded with other African tribes and with Arab merchants, exchanging gold and ivory for glass beads, cloth, and porcelain. By the 14th century, Great Zimbabwe was firmly established as the capital of a loose federation of tribes fanning out across much of the sur-

The ruins of the Great Zimbabwe stronghold, including the Great Enclosure (left) are a testament to the prominence of the ancient Shona.

rounding country. However, by the beginning of the 15th century, Great Zimbabwe had fallen into decline. Because so few written or oral records have survived from the era, its decline remains unexplained.

Around that time, a Shona *mambo*, or king, named Mutata Nyatsimba moved the seat of the empire farther north to take better advantage of the gold trade. The subsequent lineage of kings who traced their ancestry to Mutata became known as the Mutapa Dynasty.

ARRIVAL OF THE PORTUGUESE

In 1502, Vasco da Gama and other Portuguese explorers landed at Sofala, on the east coast of what is now Mozambique. The initial Portuguese excursions were met by hostile locals who were still loyal to the Arabs and strongly organized under the Mutapa Dynasty. Over the next few hundred years, however, the Mutapa state was weakened by internal struggles. Taking advantage of this civil unrest, the Portuguese were able to make greater inroads.

Although there was sporadic fighting between the Muslims and Portuguese Christian traders in the region, the first half of the 16th century was generally a peaceful time, marked by healthy competition among the traders. That ended in 1561, when Goncalo da Silveira, a missionary priest, was executed. Upon discovering that the Swahili traders had instigated for Silveira's murder, the Portuguese launched a brutal military campaign against the Muslims. In the following years, there was a major decrease in Arab trading in the region.

For a century after this campaign, the Mutapa kings collected taxes from the Portuguese, in exchange for which Portuguese traders were granted jurisdiction over trade in the kingdom. Around 1690, the era of Portuguese domination finally ended when Changamire Dombo I, ruler of the Rozwi chiefdom from the southern region of present-day Zimbabwe, drove out the Europeans.

THE CRUSHING

Although the Rozwi managed to keep the European powers at bay during much of the 18th century, they were unable to prevent revolt from within. Instability within the empire was greatly accelerated by a period of change between 1817 and 1828 known as the *Mfecane* (literally, "the crushing"). Breakaway armies from Shaka's Zulu legions swept north. One was an Ndebele army under the command of Mzilikazi. In the 1820s and 1830s, Mzilikazi's warriors mounted a series of increasingly more devastating raids of existing kingdoms, stealing cattle and causing unrest.

By 1838, the warriors had sacked Great Zimbabwe, dominated much of the country, and established a new capital in the Matopo Hills near Gubuluwayo (present-day Bulawayo). Thereafter the land essentially became divided between Mashonaland (to the north/northeast) and Matabeleland (to the south/southeast). On the edges of these regions, an assortment of smaller groups and local chieftains continued to fight for independence and challenge any notions of a unified kingdom.

THE BRITISH ARE COMING

Great Britain's interest in the region first developed in 1859, when Robert Moffat of the London Missionary Society convinced Mzilikazi to let him found a mission at Inyati. During a hunting expedition, another Englishman recognized the remains of old Shona mining operations, and invited German geologist Karl Mauch to investigate. Mauch confirmed the presence of gold and spread the news in Europe. He also surveyed the ruins at Great Zimbabwe and further captivated the world's interest with descriptions and drawings.

While Mauch grabbed the attention of prospectors and Moffat recruited missionaries, it was Moffat's son-in-law, the explorer David Livingstone, who sparked the general interest of Europeans to the region. His much-publicized journey into the interior led to the exploration of Victoria Falls in 1855.

Scottish explorer David Livingstone (1813–1873) journeyed to Victoria Falls in 1855. News of his expedition stirred European interest in Zimbabwe.

Following Mzilikazi's death in 1868, his second son, Lobengula, assumed the throne and, for a time, continued his father's policy of signing treaties with Europeans. One of the most pivotal of these was called the Rudd Concession, signed in 1888. Charles Rudd was an emissary of Cecil John Rhodes, an extremely ambitious and wealthy entrepreneur whose dream was to extend the British Empire in Africa from the southern Cape to Cairo, Egypt. In the Zimbabwe region, he sought control of mineral wealth in order to outflank the Afrikaner capitalists, who by that point had settled in the Transvaal province, located in the northeast region of South Africa.

The English version of the Rudd Concession, signed by King Lobengula, and the oral version translated to him through an interpreter were two very different documents. The former included much more land and granted Rhodes exclusive mining rights in Lobengula's domain. By the time Lobengula realized he had been tricked, it was too late to do much about it.

Rhodes and his associates used the Rudd Concession to secure a Royal Charter from the British monarchy in 1889. He then formed the British South Africa Company (BSAC) and began to recruit men into his so-called Pioneer Column, a small regiment formed to survey a path through the African bush. This group of settlers, policemen, and African mercenaries set out from eastern Botswana in June 1890. They arrived at Masvingo by the end of the month, where they raised the Union Jack and established Fort Victoria. By September they had built another fort at Salisbury (now Harare). The following year, Britain declared the country, which the settlers had already named Rhodesia after the famous entrepreneur, a British colony.

The English businessman Cecil John Rhodes (1853–1902) established the British colony of Rhodesia in the late 19th century. Rhodes wanted to expand British control of southern Africa to protect his diamond mining interests.

As more and more settlers arrived, the BSAC began to push native Africans off the best land and onto smaller and more blighted patches of middleveld and lowveld that supported few crops. Over the course of 40 years, the settlers veiled their imperialist motives by assigning these lands a series of pleasant-sounding titles—"Native Reserves," then "Tribal Trust Lands," and finally "Communal Areas."

The settlers also imposed a "hut tax" that forced blacks to work for them at very low wages. After the Ndebele had long made their living by raiding Shona farms, they now found themselves facing brutal reprisals by the BSAC, which used the raids as a justification for waging the Ndebele War in 1893. Despite losing a key battle on the banks of the Shangani River, the better-armed and organized British troops routed the Ndebele and sent Lobengula fleeing into the wilderness, where he died.

THE WARS OF LIBERATION

The BSAC's offensive practices, such as taking the best land from native Africans and doling it out to white settlers, eventually drove the Ndebele to wage an insurrection in 1896. A year later, the Shona launched their own uprising. These conflicts, known as the first *chimurenga* (war of liberation), failed to dislodge the BSAC from power.

In 1899, the region was renamed Southern Rhodesia to differentiate it from Northern Rhodesia (now Zambia). The BSAC continued to govern Southern Rhodesia with racist, exploitative laws, such as the Native Regulations, which required all blacks to carry identification papers. Those who didn't have their papers were fined, jailed, or forced to work in labor camps. In 1923, the white settlers voted not to become part of South Africa, and Southern Rhodesia became a self-governing British colony.

Only whites were allowed to serve in the new Parliament, and segregation was strictly enforced, first by the Land Apportionment Act of 1930 and then the Land Tenure Act of 1969. Both laws officially set aside huge tracts of the best land for whites, who comprised only 2 percent of the population. Unfair taxes and labor laws forced more and more blacks into indentured servitude. Moreover, voting privileges were only granted to those who could boast a degree of wealth and education virtually unattainable by native Africans.

THE FEDERATION AND THE RESISTANCE MOVEMENT

From 1953 to 1963, Southern Rhodesia formed a Federation with Northern Rhodesia and Nyasaland. In addition to rampant industrialization, this period saw the burgeoning of an organized resistance movement among educated blacks. Numerous groups expanded, such as the ANC (African National Congress), led by Joshua Nkomo. The white government was quick to ban the ANC, but its leaders just as swiftly reorganized under new names. The ANC was replaced by the NDP (National Democratic Party) in 1960, which was then replaced by the ZAPU (Zimbabwe African People's Union). Several members of ZAPU, including future president Robert Mugabe, clashed with Nkomo. They favored a more militant approach and left the organization to form ZANU (Zimbabwe African National Union).

After the Federation collapsed in 1963, most of the Ndebele aligned with the ZAPU party, while the Shona dominated ZANU. The long-standing enmity between these peoples, coupled with strong disagreements over goals and tactics, ultimately split the resistance movement. ZAPU and ZANU each formed military wings (respectively, the Zimbabwe People's Revolutionary Army, or ZIPRA, and the Zimbabwe African National Liberation Army, or ZANLA).

Black uprisings in Northern Rhodesia and Nyasaland had caused the Federation to break up and convinced the British government to recognize

Zambia (Northern Rhodesia) and Malawi (Nyasaland) as independent nations ruled by their black majorities. Eager to prevent a similar coup, the whites of Southern Rhodesia (who soon dropped the *Southern* and became simply Rhodesia again) rallied around their primary party, the Rhodesian Front (RF). In 1964, the RF's new prime minister, the ultraconservative Ian Smith, arrested many of the resistance leaders and attempted to convince Britain to give Rhodesia sovereign status. Opposed to Rhodesia's racist system, Britain refused, but in 1965 Smith forced the situation by proclaiming the Universal Declaration of Independence. Britain, the United States, and eventually the United Nations imposed economic sanctions in an effort to gain some political leverage, but Smith and the RF remained steadfast. ZANLA and ZIPRA responded by launching a guerrilla war against the government.

Zimbabwe African Peoples' Union president Joshua Nkomo (at desk, left) and secretary Washington Malianga speak to the United Nations about their struggle against the white government in Southern Rhodesia, March 1962.

THE SECOND CHIMURENGA

During the 15-year-long civil war that led to Zimbabwe's liberation, numerous atrocities were committed on both sides. The forces of the Rhodesian Front were particularly brutal, wiping out whole villages in an effort to suppress public support for the rebels.

In 1969, Smith's government offered a deal that would have granted blacks eight of 66 seats in Parliament. Unsurprisingly, the offer was refused and the resistance continued. For the next six years, the rebels were too scattered to mount much of a campaign. However, in 1975, the victories in wars for liberation in Angola and Mozambique served as a turning point. The neighboring countries now permitted Zimbabwean guerrilla forces to operate and coordinate attacks from bases within their borders.

Meanwhile, Nkomo and Mugabe, who were released from prison in a 1974 ceasefire agreement, temporarily united ZAPU, ZANU, and their respective armies to form the Patriotic Front in 1976. Smith began to feel that this combined force was a viable threat. Also, the pressure that the international community had placed on the prime minister throughout the war was strong. The economic sanctions against Rhodesia, enforced by superpowers like the United States, had their intended effect of isolating the country. Even the white-ruled government of South Africa, under pressure from the U.S. government, refused to officially recognize Smith's government.

By 1979, Smith realized that he had no other option and agreed to hold multiracial elections. However, he managed to persuade ANC chairman Bishop Abel Muzorewa and another prominent leader named Ndabaningi

The conflict in Southern Rhodesia led tens of thousands of people to flee the country during the 1970s. This photo shows young refugees at a camp in Doroi, Mozambique, 1977.

Sithole to agree to a total of 28 Parliament seats for blacks. Muzorewa was elected prime minister that year, but his concession to Smith lost him the respect of his peers, leaving Nkomo and Mugabe to become the true heroes of the liberation movement. In December, British prime minister Margaret Thatcher invited all the major players to what became known as the Lancaster House Conference, at which they tried to negotiate a more realistic constitution.

In the end, the terms of representation were basically reversed from what existed before—whites only got 20 seats out of 100. A new election was held in April 1980, in which Mugabe was made prime minister, Nkomo became minister of Home Affairs, and another prominent ZANU figure, Reverend Canaan Banana, was given the figurehead position of president. On April 18, the newly renamed Republic of Zimbabwe officially received its independence from Great Britain.

A SHORT-LIVED PEACE

The people of Zimbabwe had little time to celebrate their independence before hostilities between ZANU and ZAPU boiled over into bloodshed. The discovery of a ZAPU arms supply convinced Mugabe that his rivals were planning a coup, so he kicked the ZAPU ministers out of Parliament, seized their assets, and arrested their military leaders. Nkomo fled the country, and Mugabe sent his Fifth Brigade into Matabeleland, where it indiscriminately massacred at least 32,000 Ndebele villagers.

In 1985, ZANU increased its position in Parliament and Mugabe revealed his Five-Year Plan to convert Zimbabwe to socialism. Two years later, Mugabe abolished the position of prime minister and established an executive presidency in its place. Following Canaan Banana's resignation, Mugabe became head of state and commander of Zimbabwe's armed forces.

That same year, in an effort to end hostilities between ZANU and ZAPU, Mugabe signed the Unity Accord with Joshua Nkomo. The agreement merged the two parties (into ZANU-PF), gave amnesty to dissidents, and amended Zimbabwe's constitution to provide for up to two vice presidencies, one of which was filled by Nkomo. In 1990, a new party emerged called the Zimbabwe Unity Movement (ZUM), led by Edgar Tekere. Despite mounting a strong campaign, ZUM was soundly defeated by ZANU-PF in elections marred by vote tampering, intimidation, and violence, including an assassination attempt on Tekere. Every election since has been similarly compromised.

In 1992, the Land Acquisition Act was passed, which instituted a program through which the government would buy land from white farmers and redistribute it to Zimbabwe's black majority. From the beginning, the process was rife with corruption. In contradiction to the socialist doctrine they espoused, government officials and other wealthy blacks secretly began to snatch up the best land, while the rest of the population quickly grew disillusioned. Beginning in February 2000, war veterans eager for their piece of the pie began to forcibly occupy farms and sometimes kill white landowners. Mugabe openly supported such actions.

SIGNS OF CHANGE

In early 2000, following the death of Vice President Joshua Nkomo, Mugabe put a referendum before the country. The people voted on whether Mugabe should be made president for life and be granted the power to dissolve Parliament and declare war whenever he wished. The referendum failed by a fairly narrow margin, but enough of one to suggest a new wave of opposition was mounting against Mugabe.

Later that year, voters in the parliamentary elections gave 57 seats to members of the Movement for Democratic Change (MDC), a party formed in 1999. Presidential elections held in March 2002 were again plagued by allegations of vote manipulation and violence against the supporters of the MDC candidate, Morgan Tsvangirai. In the end, Mugabe was re-elected with 56 percent of the vote, though there were many doubts about the election's accuracy and fairness.

In March of 2008, the people of Zimbabwe held joint presidential and parliamentary elections. The results, which took more than a month to be tallied and then recounted, again proved controversial. The MDC won a majority of

Morgan Tsvangirai (left), leader of the Movement for Democratic Change (MDC) of Zimbabwe, meets with United Nations Secretary-General Ban Ki-moon in Ghana, 2008.

seats in Parliament, and Tsvangirai beat Mugabe in the general election, but not by the margin dictated by Zimbabwean law to earn him the presidency. A run-off election was scheduled for June, but Tsvangirai withdrew, once again citing violence against his supporters and a lack of faith in the fairness of the process. Mugabe won the presidency by default, but critics within Zimbabwe and around the globe questioned the legitimacy of his victory.

The flawed elections of 2008 settled nothing and in fact caused even greater turmoil among the people of Zimbabwe. Leaders from the neighboring countries of South Africa and Mozambique stepped in and tried to negotiate. In September of 2008, their efforts led to a power-sharing agreement or "Unity Government" in which Mugabe retained his presidency but Tsvangirai was made Prime Minister in early 2009. Wrangling continues over key political appointments as well as how to best implement their joint leadership.

(Opposite) President Robert Mugabe, who first took office in 1980, has received heavy criticism for human rights abuses and a land distribution program that has favored a select few. (Right) Many Zimbabweans, like these demonstrators, also accuse Mugabe of violence against dissidents and of ignoring the country's AIDS crisis.

3 A Work in Progress

ZIMBABWE'S GOVERNMENT IS described as a parliamentary democracy, though given President Mugabe's oppressive tactics, observers argue that it is more like a dictatorship. Since independence, Mugabe has used his power to force decisions by Zimbabwe's courts and legislature. Under Zimbabwe's constitution, ratified in 1979, these branches of government are supposed to be free to make certain decisions independently. In theory, the 2008 power-sharing agreement that established Mugabe's rival Morgan Tsvangirai as prime minister may create greater freedom in Zimbabwe. However, to date real change has not been apparent.

Zimbabwe's government, as dictated by its ever-changing constitution, resembles a blend of the U.S. and British systems. As in Britain, the legislative branch is known as Parliament, but its composition has changed several times over the last 30 years. From 1980 to 1987, Zimbabwe's Parliament was bicameral, meaning it had two main bodies, called the House of Assembly and the Senate. In September 1987, the Senate was abolished and Parliament became unicameral for the next 18 years. Following the parliamentary elections of 2005, the ZANU-PF majority in the House of Assembly amended the constitution and again reconstituted the Senate, in an effort to further consolidate power. Today, both legislative bodies are primarily comprised of elected officials from constituencies around the country, with a scattering of traditional chiefs and provincial governors or other presidential appointments.

Zimbabwe's judicial system, as established in 1990 by the Customary Law and Local Courts Act, comprises a standard *hierarchy* of courts, with a nod to tribal traditions at its lowest levels. The highest ruling body is the Supreme Court, which has only one chief justice and three judges of appeal. Next in line is the High Court, with 10 judges. Together these two bodies make up the Superior Courts. The Inferior Courts handle more local cases and reflect a more traditional system. Beneath the level of magistrates, rural courts are presided over by tribal chiefs and "headmen."

THE EXECUTIVE BRANCH

The highest level of Zimbabwe's executive branch currently includes the president, a vice president, a prime minister, and two deputy prime ministers. Aiding this five-member team in the governing of the nation is a pyramid network of committees and councils whose members become more numerous further down the chain of authority. A 49-member Politburo falls directly under the executive leadership, but negotiations continue within the recently constituted Unity Government over which positions will be appointed by whom. Under the Politburo is the 150-member Central Committee. Much like the presidential cabinet, these offices of the executive branch are directly tied to the current administration and can be replaced when a new president assumes power.

On the tier below the Central Committee is the Consultative Council, which is a gathering of elders and war veterans who meet twice a year to give advice to the Central Committee. Next is the Women's League and the Youth League, and below them are ten Provincial Councils, elected every three years at provincial congresses. Each Provincial Council has 71 members divided among a main wing, a women's wing, and a youth wing. Last, and certainly least in terms of power, are the District Councils, which consist of at least 5,000 members and are further subdivided into 500-member branches and 100-member cells or village committees.

When Mugabe and the ZANU-PF leaders receive charges of running a *totalitarian* government, they point to its multi-tiered administration as evidence of its "ultra-democratic" governance. In reality, few outside the party's upper ranks wield any real power.

POLITICAL ABUSES

One demonstration of the party's authoritarian control occurred in 1997, when Mugabe swiftly dismissed the National Constitutional Commission (NCC). Made up of 40 nongovernmental organizations, labor unions, and political parties, the commission ultimately had called for a new constitution that would limit the power of the executive presidency. Instead of allowing the NCC to handle the review process, Mugabe appointed his own 400-member commission, whose eventual report left his totalitarian powers intact. Mugabe then used those powers, without consulting his own commission, to add an amendment to the constitution that made it possible to seize white-owned land without providing any compensation. This move made him popular with the war veterans and helped secure him votes in the 2000 and 2002 elections.

Another of Mugabe's antidemocratic moves came early in 2003, when he arrested the mayor of Harare, Elias Mudzuri, for organizing a resistance against the ruling ZANU-PF. The cities of Harare and Bulawayo make up

During the 2008 African Union summit in Sharm el Sheikh, Egypt, the AU's executive council focused on the country's election crisis and the Mugabe regime's history of human-rights abuses. A number of African leaders wanted to take strong action by suspending Zimbabwe from the AU. However, the executive council ultimately declined to impose sanctions against Mugabe's government.

two of Zimbabwe's administrative regions (eight provinces comprise the other regions) and the citizens of both cities had elected candidates representing the MDC, the main rival to Mugabe's ZANU-PF party. Mudzuri, an outspoken opponent of Mugabe, was taken into custody in January 2003 and replaced by a deputy mayor who promptly left the MDC party and joined the ZANU-PF. In early 2004, Mugabe began reorganizing the administrations of Harare and Bulawayo by handpicking ZANU-PF governors to oversee them. In April of 2005, Mugabe further weakened his opposition in Harare by launching Operation Restore Order, which resulted in the destruction of 700,000 homes and businesses, most of them owned by poor supporters of the MDC.

Mugabe has disrupted the Republic of Zimbabwe's original democratic agenda through a strategy based primarily on bribery and the intimidation of political opponents. The president suppresses many of his enemies through Zimbabwe's security police, the Central Intelligence Organization, which uses brutal yet effective methods. Mugabe also uses sources of executive power written into Zimbabwe's constitution to his advantage. These include the power to choose much of the leadership of all three branches, and the freedom to serve an unlimited number of terms, each a lengthy six-year period. With this great authority, Mugabe has been able to stay in power for over two decades and continually make unpopular decisions without fear of his immediate removal.

Although Zimbabwe faces persistent economic decline, there is great potential in the land's rich soil, which produces crops such as sugar, corn, coffee, tea, and tobacco. (Opposite) A woman takes her infant along while she works on the farm. (Right) Customers inspect tobacco at an exchange in Harare.

4 An Economy in Crisis

ZIMBABWE SHOULD BE an affluent country today. It has an abundant supply of natural resources, a relatively sound *infrastructure*, a vast amount of land blessed with rich soil and perfect growing conditions, and, with its many natural attractions and wildlife preserves, a potentially huge tourist draw. For much of the 19th and 20th centuries, the country's economy thrived, thanks to its agricultural exports and a robust mining industry.

However, the wealth it produced in those years was held by a tiny minority of whites who controlled the government and owned all the businesses and farms. Zimbabwe's economy started to falter in the 1960s, when black nationalists began to ferment the revolution that eventually led to the overthrow of the white minority. During the brutal 15-year civil war that followed, many white farmers and other business owners fled the country or fell victim to civil unrest. Those who remained had difficulty maintaining their operations. The result was an extended disruption in production at all levels of the economy.

Following independence, the new government embarked on a Five-Year Plan to socialize the country and convert independently owned businesses into state-run cooperatives. This plan ultimately proved unsuccessful. The government spent too much money subsidizing collective businesses, whose efficiency was low due to a lack of proper training and education among the new managers. Frustrated by the new system, white farmers continued their exodus, further compromising the farming industry. The national debt grew huge and inflation soared. To make matters worse, the country experienced an extended drought throughout the first half of the 1990s. Crops failed, cattle died, and famine broke out.

Robert Mugabe, at that time the prime minister, sought aid from the international community and received loans in exchange for promises to cut spending, control inflation, and convert the country back to capitalism. Policies like the Economic Structural Adjustment Program, instituted in 1991, and the Millennium Economic Recovery Program of 2001 were designed to achieve those ends. However, their effectiveness has been hampered by the government's inability to implement them.

During this period of rising inflation, President Mugabe made several policy decisions that further ravaged the economy and isolated his country from the rest of the world. The first was to spend hundreds of millions of dollars to help President Laurent Kabila suppress widespread rebellion in the Democratic Republic of the Congo. The second was to continue enforcing the land redistribution program, which either bought or (more commonly) seized property from white farmers and gave it to ZANU-PF leaders or the *squatters* who forcibly occupied the land. This chaotic and corruption-riddled redistribution of the country's most important resource has only injured an already damaged economy.

Mugabe's disastrous policies, coupled with his human rights abuses and manipulation of election results, have led to international condemnation. The International Monetary Fund has threatened multiple times to expel the country completely, and numerous nations around the world have instituted

THE ECONOMY OF ZIMBABWE

Gross domestic product (GDP*): $4.27 billion (166th)

Economic growth rate: 5.9%

Inflation: 134.5% (2002 est.)

Natural resources: coal, chromium ore, asbestos, gold, nickel, copper, iron ore, vanadium, lithium, tin, platinum group metals

Agriculture (19.5% of GDP): corn, cotton, tobacco, wheat, coffee, sugarcane, peanuts, sheep, goats, pigs

Industry (24% of GDP): mining (coal, gold, platinum, copper, nickel, tin, diamonds, clay, numerous metallic and nonmetallic ores), steel; wood products, cement, chemicals, fertilizer, clothing and footwear, foodstuffs, beverages

Services (56.5% of GDP): government, other

Foreign Trade:

Exports—$2.54 billion: platinum, cotton, tobacco, gold, ferroalloys, textiles/clothing

Imports—$4.04 billion: machinery and transport equipment, other manufactures, chemicals, fuels, food products

Currency exchange rate: U.S. $1 = 361 Zimbabwean dollars

*GDP is the total value of goods and services produced in a country annually.
All figures are 2010 estimates unless otherwise indicated.
Sources: CIA World Factbook, 2011.

economic sanctions against Mugabe and his allies in an effort to pressure them into governing more democratically.

Rampant disease epidemics have also taken a toll on the country's workforce. Today, nearly 15 percent of adult Zimbabweans are infected with HIV or AIDS. In addition, during 2008 and 2009 widespread outbreaks of cholera further ravaged the populace. These epidemics have eradicated much of the country's workforce and drastically declined economic output.

All of the factors mentioned above have left Zimbabwe in a state of acute financial crisis. In 2007, economic officials tried to slow down what had become the world's worst rate of inflation by devaluing the currency by 1,200 percent. To put this in perspective, overnight the rate of exchange for one U.S. dollar increased from 250 to 30,000 Zimbabwean dollars. The government also began to print banknotes in formerly unimaginable denominations, such as a $50 billion bill. Unfortunately, these efforts did little to help and the hyperinflation continued. In 2009, businesses were instructed by then-

Now-defunct Zimbabwean currency, including $25 billion, $50 billion, and $100 billion bills.

A health worker at a clinic in Nyakomba, Zimbabwe, teaches primary school students about HIV infection and AIDS. Zimbabwe's economic output has drastically declined in part because a large percentage of the working-age population is infected with HIV or AIDS.

finance minister Patrick Chinamasa to begin accepting more stable currencies from foreign countries, such as the U.S. dollar or the South African rand. This drastic move effectively ended hyperinflation. However, until significant change occurs, Zimbabwe has officially abandoned its own currency.

In 2011, the country began to see its first signs of economic growth in more than a decade. Although international sanctions remain in place, there is hope that if Mugabe and Tsvangirai achieve some measure of cooperation, the sanctions will be lifted and a more stable economy will follow.

AGRICULTURE

Historically, commercial farming has been the single most important industry in Zimbabwe. In addition to feeding and employing much of the nation, agricul-

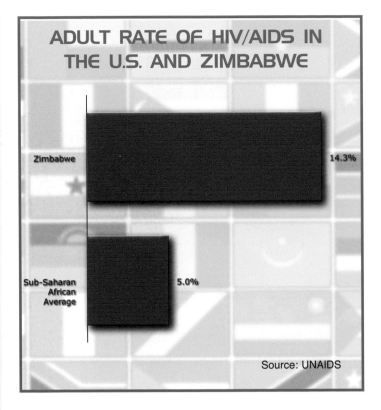

ADULT RATE OF HIV/AIDS IN THE U.S. AND ZIMBABWE

Zimbabwe — 14.3%

Sub-Saharan African Average — 5.0%

Source: UNAIDS

tural products—including sugar, tobacco, cotton, corn, coffee, and tea—accounted for a considerable share of Zimbabwe's exports during much of the 20th century.

Since independence, however, the land that has been returned to landless blacks has mostly been used for *subsistence farming*. Setting aside the complex moral and legal issues surrounding this practice, subsistence farming neither grows enough food to feed the rest of the nation nor creates products for export. While it is true that many collective farms have been established to fill the role of the white-owned commercial farms, so far they have not been able to match the levels of production and efficiency required to meet the country's needs. Several years of drought have further hampered their efforts.

Agriculture still provides about 19 percent of the gross domestic product and 40 percent of export earnings, but much of that income is derived from the sale of tobacco. Today, Zimbabwe is the seventh-largest producer in the world. It is more difficult to determine exactly how many Zimbabweans work on farms or support themselves through subsistence farming. However, given that two-thirds of the population live in rural areas, where cattle and crops provide the only true economy and means of sustenance, the importance of farming to the nation's welfare cannot be overstated.

MINING

If agriculture fueled the engine of Zimbabwe's modern history, mining primed the pump and sparked the ignition. Extracted from the Iron Age onward, gold is what inspired the Shona's first contact with the Arabs, what attracted the Portuguese, and what first caught the attention of entrepreneur Cecil Rhodes. Although it was once commonly held that all those years of mining had depleted the country's reserve, a boom in the mid-1990s proved such fears were unfounded. The problem now is maintaining production amid political turmoil and economic collapse. Over 22,000 kilograms of gold were mined in 1995, but only 5,000 in 2009. That drop represents an annual loss of nearly a half billion dollars.

Much work remains to restore high productivity, but there is no denying that Zimbabwe's natural resources have the potential to turn its economy around. Diamonds in particular represent a huge potential windfall. Unfortunately, there is a long history of brutal work conditions and inequality associated with mining in Zimbabwe, particularly at the diamond fields of Marange. Initially, this involved white owners exploiting black workers, but more recently, military officers charged with guarding the mines have committed atrocities against workers and independent miners. In November of 2009, the Kimberly Process placed a ban on diamonds mined in Zimbabwe. This international initiative attempts to prevent diamond profits

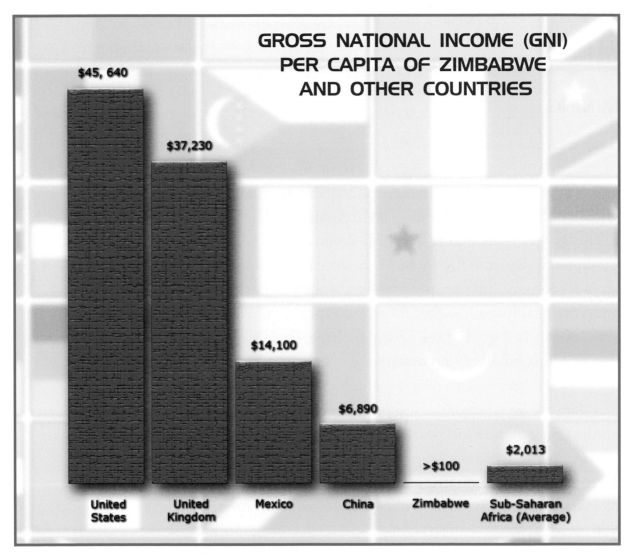

GROSS NATIONAL INCOME (GNI)
PER CAPITA OF ZIMBABWE
AND OTHER COUNTRIES

$45, 640 — United States
$37,230 — United Kingdom
$14,100 — Mexico
$6,890 — China
>$100 — Zimbabwe
$2,013 — Sub-Saharan Africa (Average)

Gross national income per capita is the total value of all goods and services produced domestically in a year, supplemented by income received from abroad, divided by midyear population. The above figures take into account fluctuations in currency exchange rates and differences in inflation rates across global economies, so that an international dollar has the same purchasing power as a U.S. dollar has in the United States.   Source: World Bank, 2011.

from funding armed conflicts and pressure African mining nations into conducting operations that are free from human rights violations. The ban on Marange diamonds was lifted in June of 2010. This should help Zimbabwe's economy, but debate continues over how to enrich the general populace and not just high-ranking allies of those in power.

SERVICES

Zimbabwe's remaining industries are grouped under the category of "services"—a catchall that includes everything from tourism to food sales to clothing manufacture, and which is estimated to account for 57 percent of the gross domestic product. The breakdown of law and order over the past decade has sent many of these industries into freefall, however. The tourism sector has particularly suffered. For much of the last decade, all major airlines stopped flying into Harare. In 2008, however, British Airways announced that it would begin flying to Zimbabwe again and tourism officials hope that other airlines will follow suit.

Perhaps even more economically devastating than the decrease in tourism is the inverse trend that has black business owners joining their white counterparts in a mass exodus out of the country. Not only is their departure taking wealth out of the economy, it is also robbing the country of its educated and affluent middle class. Most of Zimbabwe's blacks hardly have enough money for food and shelter, let alone the capital required to start a business or pay for an education. If the small number of blacks that are capable of investing in the marketplace continues to emigrate, the current gulf between rich and poor will only widen.

The Ndebele and Shona peoples of Zimbabwe share common ground, but also maintain distinct cultural traits. (Opposite) A traditional Ndebele home is decorated with geometric patterns. (Right) A Christian church in Harare. Christian beliefs have a strong influence even on those who practice traditional religions in Zimbabwe.

5 Descendants of the Bantu

COMPARED TO THE rest of Africa, Zimbabwe has a relatively *homogeneous* population, consisting of two main ethnic groups and only a handful of others. Excluding the tiny minorities of whites and Asians, nearly all Zimbabweans descend from the Bantu peoples who left northern Africa approximately 2,000 years ago. The vast majority—82 percent by the latest estimates—classify themselves as Shona, tracing their ancestry to the waves of migrants who first settled the eastern parts of the country in the 10th and 11th centuries.

The Shona are made up of six primary subgroups: Karanga, Zezuru, Manyika, Tonga-Korekore, Rosvi, and Ndau. Each has its own dialect, which is in turn divided into 30 sub-dialects. Standard Shona, also known as Union Shona, is a blend of them all. Despite—or perhaps because of—this array of native tongues, English has remained the official language of the country since independence.

The remaining Zimbabweans are nearly all Ndebele (currently about 14 percent) and descend from the faction of Nguni peoples who fled southern Africa during Shaka Zulu's reign and the resulting Mfecane. Although the history of conflict between the Shona and Ndebele has spurred strong animosities that manifest today, over the centuries of contact, cohabitation, and intermarriage, their cultures have found some common ground.

Traditionalists of both ethnicities believe in the god Mwari and spirit mediums, practice ancestor worship, maintain strong kinship connections, engage primarily in subsistence farming, and treat cattle as their main unit of wealth. The one substantial difference between them is linguistic—although both languages ultimately derive from Bantu, the use of "clicks" and other distinctive sounds in Ndebele make it a closer cousin to Zulu and Xhosa than Shona. The Ndebele have also historically placed a higher premium on nationalism than the more locally organized Shona, but in the last quarter-century the quest for majority rule has made nationalists of nearly all Zimbabweans.

TRADITIONAL BELIEFS

Zimbabwe has a long history of cultural *assimilation*. As new groups have arrived to the country, attractive aspects of their cultures and religions have been adopted and incorporated by resident peoples (and vice versa). The result is a blend of old and new that has enabled cultures to survive through their adaptability.

Early forms of *animism* and ancestor worship were likely practiced by the San Bushmen, as suggested by their elaborate burial sites and the depictions in rock art paintings. Animism and ancestor worship represent two of the four core tenets of the Shona religion. (The other two are a belief in spirit mediums and the worship of Mwari as the Supreme God and Creator.)

Although there is some overlap, Zimbabwean spirit mediums generally fall into two categories: *svikiro* and *n'anga*. Both communicate with the spirits of the dead, but their aims are slightly different. *Svikiros* consult with spirits that are both local (*vadzimu*) and nationally recognized (*mhondoro*) to help deliver prophetic messages and personal or political advice. *N'angas*, on the other hand, are primarily healers who negotiate with the vengeful spirits believed to cause illness.

Traditional Zimbabweans also believe in a third type of practitioner of the supernatural arts. These are the *muroyi*, or evil witches, who summon the vengeful spirits that cause unnatural illness and death. The only way to combat a *muroyi* is to enlist the services of a *n'anga*. Even today, belief in witches and mediums remains one more of the most enduring and distinctive traits of traditional Zimbabwean culture.

British colonialists, and more recently the Marxist-based Mugabe administration, have tried to stamp out such cultural holdovers with the Witchcraft Suppression Act (WSA). Originally passed in 1899, the WSA is a good example of how difficult it can be to legislate religion. In 1989, nearly 100 years later, belief in witches remained so widespread and cases of alleged witchcraft were so numerous that the government amended the Act and made it illegal to accuse anyone of being a witch. Nevertheless, the practices continued even if the government refused to acknowledge their existence or try such cases in a court of law. In 2006, the government reversed its position and again made witchcraft illegal, while also instituting laws to protect those who are groundlessly accused.

The Shona religion (and its Ndebele variant) has many rituals, and a few important ones bear mentioning. A ceremony known as a *bira* is held whenever a family wishes to enlist the spiritual aid of an ancestor. The ritual usually consists of an all-night ceremony where members consume specially brewed beer; eat a ritually slaughtered animal; and play, listen, or dance to a

THE PEOPLE OF ZIMBABWE

Population: 12,084,304
Ethnic groups: African 98% (Shona 82%, Ndebele 14%, other 2%), mixed and Asian 1%, white less than 1%
Age structure:
  0–14 years: 41.9%
  15–64 years: 54.3%
  65 years and over: 3.8%
Population growth rate: 4.31%
Birth rate: 31.86 births/1,000 population
Infant mortality rate: 29.5 deaths/1,000 live births
Death rate: 13.58 deaths/1,000 population
Total fertility rate: 3.63 children born/woman

Life expectancy at birth:
  total population: 49.64 years
  male: 49.93 years
  female: 39.34 years
Religions: syncretic (part Christian, part indigenous beliefs) 50%, Christian 25%, indigenous beliefs 24%, Muslim and other 1%
Languages: English (official), Shona, Sindebele (the language of the Ndebele, sometimes called Ndebele), numerous but minor tribal dialects
Literacy: 90.7% (2003)

All figures are 2011 estimates unless otherwise indicated.
Source: Adapted from CIA World Factbook, 2003.

particular kind of trance-inducing music (known as **mbira**). The desired result of these activities is the possession of a *svikiro* or *n'anga*, who serves as the mouthpiece for the summoned ancestor.

A number of ceremonies attend deaths. The first, called the *kuviga*, begins with the body lying in state for no more than 24 hours, followed by a funeral procession and burial. One lunar month after the funeral, a *mharadzo* (also known as *kudzira*) is held by the surviving family members to cleanse their spirits and honor the newly deceased.

Other rituals recognize marriages and property inheritance. Traditionally, a husband must pay his fiancée's family a kind of inverse dowry (called *rowara*), in exchange for guarantees of her fertility. Another tradition, called *kungara nhaka*, holds that when the husband dies, his wife and their land, cattle, and other possessions become the property of his oldest surviving brother. Recent laws, however, have mediated these practices somewhat.

THE INFLUENCE OF CHRISTIANITY

Despite its emphasis on spirit mediums and other supernatural beliefs, the Shona religion is essentially **monotheistic**, with Mwari standing as the one God and Creator. The *mhondoro* and *vadzimu* comprise a hierarchy that functions somewhat like the hierarchy of angels in certain Christian denominations.

In fact, it was partly this fundamental similarity between the two religions—together with the evangelical work of the missionaries and the Western health care and social prestige afforded by the missions and churches—that convinced so many Zimbabweans to adopt Christianity. The result is a *syncretic* blend of both Christianity and traditional beliefs to which about 50 percent of the population subscribes. An additional 25 percent follows the tenets of Christianity alone. While the Roman Catholic Church is the fastest growing of the country's traditional churches, evangelical groups are expanding at a faster rate. The remaining 25 percent mostly uphold the traditional Shona religion, or its Ndebele variant, though a fraction (about 1 percent) are Muslim, Hindu, or Jewish.

A drummer performs in Matobo National Park. Percussion instruments figure prominently in *mbira* music.

THE ARTS

Zimbabwe's primary genre of music is called *mbira* and derives from a form developed to accompany *bira* ceremonies. *Mbira* is also the name of a thumb piano that is the form's central instrument. On a sounding board, which is amplified by a resonator (typically a large gourd), metal prongs of varying lengths are mounted at an angle over a guitar-like bridge. Variations on the instrument also have shells or rattles either inside a hollow resonator, or on its surface, which produce an additional buzzing tone.

There are several types of mbira music, but the most important and the original source of all other variants is the *mbira dzavadzimu*, played to commune with ancestral spirits. Mbira ensembles may also include the marimba (a type of xylophone), the mouth harp, several types of drums, pipes, or flutes, other basic stringed instruments, and numerous kinds of rattles. The instruments are almost always accompanied by singing (often done by the players themselves), typically in a call-and-response format. The ability to improvise is highly valued and an integral part of the music.

Props like this one are used in the performance of Zimbabwean dances.

Zimbabwe has other rich traditions of dance and song. Each art form adapts in some way to changing times but still maintains a cultural continuum from one generation to the next. This continuity is reflected by the two types of traditional songs sung by the Shona: the *nyizo dzepasi* and the *chimurenga*. The timeless *nyizo dzepasi*, or "songs of the earth," accompany and help sustain the rituals surrounding ancestor worship, while the more modern *chimurenga* songs helped unite and inspire the revolutionaries before, during, and after the independence movement.

One art form that receives a good deal of international attention is Shona sculpture. Using the materials of wood and stone, sculptors depict subjects that range from gods, spirits, and ancestors to birds and reptiles. Wood-carving, basketry, and pottery are other popular art forms. With their beautiful symmetrical patterns, Shona baskets illustrate the devotion that weavers have for detail.

Though Zimbabwe's cities are expanding, many people remain in rural communities. (Opposite) Harare, the economic and political center, is by far the largest city. (Right) *Rondavels*, or round huts, are typical house structures for a majority of Zimbabweans.

6 From City to Countryside

COSMOPOLITAN DEVELOPMENT IS still fairly new to Zimbabwe and its cities are therefore small by world standards. Recent census figures indicate that about two-thirds of the country's inhabitants still live in rural areas. However, that is certain to change as the population continues to grow, the country becomes more industrialized, and more and more people move to the urban centers in search of economic opportunity.

HARARE

Known for its *jacaranda*-lined avenues, pleasant weather, and blend of international sophistication and historic charm, Harare is the capital of Zimbabwe and the seat of the country's economy and government. The city's 2004 population was an estimated 1,976,400 people—nearly double the size of Bulawayo, Zimbabwe's next-largest city.

Harare was founded in 1890, when the Pioneer Column of the BSAC arrived and built a settlement. It was dubbed Fort Salisbury after the British prime minister at the time, the Marquis of Salisbury. In 1923, when Southern Rhodesia (as Zimbabwe was then known) officially became a British colony, Salisbury was named its capital by the white settlers. In 1953, the city acquired even greater prominence as the capital of the newly formed Federation of Rhodesia and Nyasaland.

Thereafter, funds and resources from all three countries fueled a building boom in the city that continued until 1963–64. In those years, the collapse of the Federation, Prime Minister Ian Smith's internationally unpopular break with England, and the resulting economic sanctions imposed by the United Nations all contributed to a nationwide recession. Following independence in 1980, the new majority-ruled government renamed the city Harare, in honor of a local chieftain who had held power in the area prior to the Pioneer Column's arrival.

In addition to hosting Zimbabwe's primary financial institutions, sporting arenas, and international airport, Harare is also the country's center of art and learning. In 1957, the University of Zimbabwe—the first school of higher education in the Federation—was founded there. In later years the National Archives was built in the city, as were the National Gallery, Museum, and Library. Many of Zimbabwe's most accomplished artists, particularly the sculptors who make up the celebrated Shona school, live in Harare.

BULAWAYO

Although smaller than Harare, Bulawayo can boast a longer history than its northeastern sister—one more rooted in Zimbabwe's native culture and

African Unity Square is a park in Harare.

precolonial past. This connection with the past is bolstered by the city's proximity to the ancient burial grounds, rock art sites, and sacred shrines in the
Matopo Hills to the south.

The city's name (originally Gubuluwayo) means "place of slaughter" in
Ndebele—a frank reference to the brutal series of battles among rival chief-
doms that bloodied the region throughout the 19th century. Bulawayo was
ultimately rebuilt by the British and achieved its place as a hub of industry
and trade when it became the major stop along the railway line from
Capetown, South Africa, to Salisbury.

Following independence, Bulawayo again saw internal fighting among black Zimbabweans as it was the home base of ZAPU and the Ndebele insurrection, as well as the site of Mugabe's most brutal reprisals. These days, Bulawayo continues to be a center of export, particularly in textiles, but it strives to broaden its reputation beyond its manufacturing exploits. There are many cultural and historical attractions in the city to help achieve this goal, such as the National University of Science and Technology, the National History Museum (home to one of Africa's largest collections), the nearby Khami Ruins (the second-largest archaeological site in the country, after Great Zimbabwe), and Matobo National Park.

CHITUNGWIZA AND MUTARE

Zimbabwe's third-largest city, Chitungwiza, is technically not a city at all, but a sprawling satellite of Harare. Formerly known as Seke, it was established by Ian Smith in 1977 in an effort to redirect some of the migrants flooding the capital. Now with a 2004 population of roughly 423,800 people, it has earned the status of a metropolitan area.

On the eastern border with Mozambique, in the shadow of the Vumba Mountains, lies Mutare, the country's fourth-largest city and capital of the Manicaland province. Until 1982, it was known as Umtali (a European corruption of its current name). Its population (estimated at 195,300 in 2004) is comprised of nearly all Shona. Local game preserves, upscale resorts, ample hiking trails, and a picturesque mountain setting all make Mutare a popular destination among tourists, especially those on their way to Mozambique and the Indian Ocean. However, its provincial location and the lingering effects of the devastation wrought by war present significant obstacles for its future growth.

OTHER CITIES

Two more cities of note—Gweru and Kwekwe—are situated smack-dab in the middle of Zimbabwe, about 37 miles (60 km) apart. Gweru (formerly Gwelo), with about 157,000 inhabitants in 2004, is twice as large as Kwekwe, but both benefit by being on the main highway between Harare and Bulawayo. Both also owe much of their early development to lucrative crops and the presence of gold and other valuable minerals in the region.

Gweru is the capital of the Midlands province; its name is believed to have originated from a word describing the steep, sloping nature of the surrounding countryside. Kwekwe's origins are a bit more poetic, as the name is said to derive from the sounds made by the frogs of its namesake river. Long spelled as *Que Que*, the city's name was officially changed during the wave of name changes that swept the nation after independence.

Relatively small in terms of population (83,300 in 2004), but huge in symbolic and historical significance, Masvingo was officially founded in 1890. Then known as Fort Victoria, it was the second outpost built by the Pioneer Column, and thereafter served as both a critical stopover for settlers en route to Salisbury and the headquarters for local mining and farming operations. But Masvingo's true import, at least to the native peoples, lies in its proximity to the site of Great Zimbabwe—inspiration, namesake, and ancestral capital of the modern nation.

A CALENDAR OF ZIMBABWEAN FESTIVALS

With 25 percent of its population practicing Christianity, 24 percent upholding traditional beliefs, and most of the remaining 51 percent believing in a personalized blend of both, Zimbabwe is a model of cross-cultural spirituality. The number of religious holidays officially recognized by the government, however, is relatively few. In their place are important civic remembrances in which the entire nation can participate.

January

New Year's Day festivities fall on January 1 and the evening prior, as in most other countries. People celebrate in hotels, restaurants, and public squares.

April

April 18, **Independence Day**, commemorates the day in 1980 when the Republic of Zimbabwe was officially recognized as a sovereign nation by Great Britain. At the end of April or beginning of May, Zimbabwe's capital city hosts the **Harare International Festival of the Arts (HIFA)**, a celebration of the four main art fields—music, theater, fine arts, and dance—in Zimbabwe and the rest of southern Africa.

May

May 1 is **Worker's Day**, which like Labor Day in the United States, recognizes the country's working people.

May 25, **Africa Day**, marks the anniversary of the formation of the Organization of African Unity (OAU), a continental organization promoting cooperation and prosperity (a similar organization, the African Union, replaced the OAU in 2002).

August

Heroes' Days run August 11–12; the first day honors specific heroes of the independence movement and the second day (sometimes called **Defense Forces Day**) is dedicated to the armed forces as a whole.

December

December 6 is **National Tree Planting Day**. Proclaimed shortly after independence by Mugabe, this day raises awareness of the need for sustainable forestry practices, particularly among the nation's youth.

On **Unity Day**, December 22, Zimbabweans celebrate their differences and recognize their common ties.

Christmas is celebrated on December 25, just like everywhere else, but on December 26 Zimbabweans also celebrate **Boxing Day**. This is a British holiday that traditionally served as an excuse to give servants, who typically worked on Christmas, the following day off.

A CALENDAR OF ZIMBABWEAN FESTIVALS

Christian Observances

Zimbabwe's Christians observe holy days on particular days each year, but many other major celebrations are held according to a lunar calendar, in which the months correspond to the phases of the moon. A lunar month is shorter than a typical month of the Western calendar. Therefore, the festival dates vary from year to year. Other celebrations are observed seasonally.

The major Christian festivals on the lunar cycle involve the suffering and death of Jesus Christ. **Ash Wednesday** marks the start of a period of self-sacrifice called **Lent**, which lasts for 40 days. The final eight days of Lent are known as **Holy Week**. A number of important days are observed, including **Palm Sunday**, which commemorates Jesus' arrival in Jerusalem; **Holy Thursday**, which marks the night of the Last Supper; **Good Friday**, the day of Jesus' death on the cross; and **Easter Monday**, which marks his resurrection. (In Western countries, Easter is typically celebrated on the day before.)

RECIPES

Amboli (Thin Porridge)

Millet, flour
Flour, wheat (fermented)
Water

Directions:
1. Mix millet flour with water to make a fine paste. Add a small quantity of fermented flour, stirring. Keep the mix for one day in a warm place.
2. Add the mix to boiling water and stir constantly to obtain a porridge of free-flowing, creamy consistency.
3. Cool and serve.

Sadza (Cornbread Dumpling)

4 cups water
2 cups mealie-meal (or cornmeal)

Directions:
1. Bring 3 1/2 cups water to a boil and reserve 1/2 cup.
2. Make paste with 2 Tbsp. mealie-meal and the reserved cold water.
3. When water boils, pour the paste into the pot, stirring constantly to prevent lumps.
4. When smooth, cover pot and allow to boil over medium heat for 30–45 minutes.
5. Add the remainder of the mealie-meal gradually, stirring all the time to prevent lumps.

6. Cover pot, reduce heat.
7. Serve with *dovi* (see below).

Dovi (Peanut Butter Stew)

2 medium onions, finely chopped
2 Tbsp. butter
2 cloves garlic, finely sliced and crushed
1 tsp. salt and 1/2 tsp. pepper
1 chili pepper or 1/2 tsp. cayenne pepper
2 green peppers, chopped
1 chicken, cut into pieces
3 to 4 fresh tomatoes (or 1 large can of tomatoes)
6 Tbsp. smooth peanut butter
1/2 lb. spinach or pumpkin leaves

Directions:
1. In a large stew pot over medium heat, sauté onions in butter until golden brown. Add garlic, salt, and hot peppers.
2. Stir for 2 or 3 minutes then add green peppers and chicken. Brown the chicken.
3. When all the chicken pieces are brown on every side, mash tomatoes with a fork and mix them into the stew, along with about 2 cups water. Reduce heat and simmer for 5 to 10 minutes.
4. Thin the peanut butter with a few spoons of hot broth and add half the resulting paste to the pot. Simmer until the meat is well cooked.

5. In a separate pot, boil spinach or pumpkin leaves for several minutes until tender. Drain and toss with the remainder of the peanut paste. Serve stew and greens side by side.

Note: In Africa, every member of the family eats from the pot by dipping into it with corn-meal bread or chapatis.

Reprinted from *The Africa News Cookbook: Africa Cooking for Western Kitchens*, edited by Tami Hultman. New York: Penguin, 1985.

Zimbabwean Sweet Potato Cookies

(Makes four dozen cookies)
2 1/2 cups all-purpose flour
1 1/2 tsp. baking powder
1/2 tsp. baking soda
1/4 tsp. salt
1/2 cup butter or margarine (1 stick)
1/4 cup sugar
1 Tbsp. grated lemon peel
1 tsp. nutmeg
1/4 cup honey
1 egg
1 cup grated, raw sweet potatoes

Directions:
1. Preheat the oven to 350°F.
2. Sift the flour, baking powder, baking soda, and salt into a medium-size mixing bowl. Set aside.
3. Cream the butter or margarine with the sugar in a large mixing bowl. Mix in the lemon peel, nutmeg, honey, and egg. Then, stir in the grated sweet potato.
4. Blend the flour mixture into the sweet potato mixture.
5. Place rounded teaspoons of the cookie dough onto an ungreased cookie sheet. The cookies should be spaced at least 1/2-inch apart.
6. Bake for 7 minutes. Remove cookies from the sheet and cool on a rack.

Optional: Make a lemon glaze for the cookies. In a glass mixing bowl, blend 1 1/2 cups confectioners' sugar with 1 Tbsp. lemon juice and 2 tsp. water. Spread the glaze on the cooled cookies.

GLOSSARY

Afrikaner—a white native of South Africa and descendant of a Dutch settler; also known as a Boer.

animism—the doctrine that all natural objects and natural phenomena have souls.

assimilation—the process of adopting the customs and beliefs of another culture.

bush—wilderness; unspoiled nature area.

chimurenga—a war of liberation in Zimbabwe; it may refer to the failed 1896 uprising or the second revolution, begun in 1966 and ultimately leading to the fall of the white regime in 1980.

deciduous—used to describe trees and other plants that shed their leaves in autumn.

hierarchy—an organization whose members are arranged in ranks.

homogeneous—of the same or similar kind or nature.

infrastructure—the basic facilities and equipment needed for the functioning of a country or area, such as roads, railways, shipping lines, electricity, and manufacturing plants.

jacaranda—a tree common to Southern Africa (but of South American origin) known for its fragrant wood and bright purple blossoms.

kopjes—small hills rising from the African veld, often formed by an outcrop of granite.

mbira—the primary mode of music in Zimbabwe, originally developed to accompany a common ceremony called the *bira*.

Mfecane—the forced northward migration of Nguni peoples living in the eastern part of South Africa during the early 19th century.

mhondoro—means "great spirits"; ancestor spirits who are venerated on a national or tribal level.

monotheistic—characterized by the belief in only one God.

n'angas—spirit mediums who specialize in traditional healing and the exorcising of the vengeful spirits thought to cause illness and death.

squatters—in Zimbabwe, people (often veterans from the civil war) who have occupied farms that have either been abandoned by or forcibly taken from white owners.

subsistence farming—the practice of growing only enough to feed yourself or your immediate family or tribe.

svikiro—spirit mediums believed to communicate with ancestors (*vadzimu* or *mhondoro*), from whom they deliver advice or prophecy.

syncretic—characterized by the combination of different forms of belief or practice.

totalitarian—relating to a government in which a single party rules over the country without opposition.

vadzimu—ancestor spirits that are venerated locally or by members of an extended family.

veld—open country or grasslands.

watershed—a land area that drains into a particular body of water.

PROJECT AND REPORT IDEAS

Report Ideas

Write one-page biographies on any of the following people:

- Robert Mugabe
- Cecil Rhodes
- David Livingstone
- Ian Smith

Geography Map

Create a map of Zimbabwe that includes the following features:

- Bordering countries: Zambia, Mozambique, South Africa, and Botswana
- Major rivers: the Zambezi, the Limpopo, and the Sabi
- Geographic regions: the highveld, middleveld, lowveld, and Eastern Highlands
- National parks and game reserves: Hwange and Gonarezhou
- Major cities: Harare, Bulawayo, Mutare, Gweru, Kwekwe, Masvingo
- Sites of interest: Victoria Falls and Lake Kariba, Great Zimbabwe, Matopo Hills, Mount Inyangani

PROJECT AND REPORT IDEAS

Writing Projects

Write a first-person account from the perspective of a 3,000-year-old baobab tree. Research one of the myths about your origins and describe what historical events you might have witnessed in Zimbabwe during your lifetime.

Pretend that you are an adventurer and have gone on a safari in Hwange National Park. Write a first-person account of your experience. Describe the landscape and all the animals you see, specifying their diets and prominent features.

If you could commune with one of your ancestors, who would it be and why? Give your answer in a one-page essay.

Write a two-part account of the Pioneer Column's arrival in Zimbabwe. For the first part, imagine yourself as a British member of the Column and describe what trials and tribulations you experienced along the way. For the second part, imagine yourself as a native black African and describe the experience of witnessing the arrival of the white settlers and what stands out about their appearance or behavior.

CHRONOLOGY

ca. 7000 B.C.	The San Bushmen leave behind famous rock paintings.
A.D. 700–800	Shona ancestors begin migrating to the region.
900–1000	The Shona build Great Zimbabwe.
ca. 1450	The Mutapa Dynasty is established.
1511–13	Portuguese explorer Antonio Fernandes travels through modern-day Zimbabwe.
1693–95	The Rozwi chiefdom expels the Portuguese from the interior.
1820–40s	The Mfecane forces the Ndebele to migrate northward into Shona territory.
1888–90	Lobengula signs the Rudd Concession, unknowingly granting exclusive mining rights to Cecil Rhodes; Rhodes forms British South Africa Company (BSAC); the Pioneer Column of the BSAC enters Zimbabwe and builds forts at Victoria (Masvingo) and Salisbury (Harare).
1891	Rhodesia is declared a British protectorate.
1893	The BSAC wages the Ndebele War.
1896	The first *chimurenga* takes place.
1923	Southern Rhodesia officially becomes a British colony.
1930	The Land Apportionment Act is passed.
1953	The Federation of Rhodesia and Nyasaland is formed.
1957–63	Various resistance groups are organized, including the African National Congress (ANC), the Zimbabwe Africa People's Union (ZAPU), and the Zimbabwe African National Union (ZANU).
1964–65	Ian Smith becomes prime minister, and arrests many resistance leaders.
1966	ZANLA, the military arm of ZANU, initiates civil war.
1974	Smith signs temporary cease-fire agreement, releasing many revolutionary leaders from jail, including Robert Mugabe and Joshua Nkomo.
1978–79	General elections are held; Bishop Abel Muzorewa becomes prime minister; following the Lancaster House Conference, a new Zimbabwe constitution is drafted.
1980	Mugabe becomes prime minister; Zimbabwe is officially granted independence.
1982	Nkomo is accused of plotting a coup and flees country; the government arrests ZAPU

military leaders and massacres Ndebele villagers.

1987	ZAPU and ZANU join together and become ZANU-PF; Mugabe makes himself president.
1992	The Land Acquisition Act is passed.
1998	Mugabe supports the Democratic Republic of the Congo's suppression of an internal rebellion, putting severe strain on the faltering economy.
1999	The Movement for Democratic Change (MDC) is formed.
2000	Mugabe floats referendum to become president for life, but the people reject it; the MDC wins 57 seats in Parliament.
2002	Mugabe retains presidency in rigged election; exodus of white farmers and corrupt land redistribution program results in food shortages, economic breakdown, and rampant inflation.
2005	ZANU-PF wins parliamentary elections, despite protests from opposition groups; Operation Restore Order leaves 700,000 homeless in Harare.
2007	Zimbabwe devalues its currency 1,200 percent in an effort to curb inflation.
2008	MDC wins control of Parliament in March elections; Mugabe retains presidency when Morgan Tsvangirai withdaws from the election, claiming widespread fraud by the government; cholera epidemic induces national emergency.
2009	Tsvangirai sworn in as Prime Minister as part of a power-sharing agreement with Mugabe; Zimbabwe abandons its own currency to halt hyperinflation.
2010	Tsvangirai calls for international sanctions to be lifted in support of the Unity Government.
2011	In June, the Southern African Development Community (SADC) holds a regional summit on Zimbabwe after determining that ZANU-PF had failed to implement key sections of the political power-sharing agreement.
2012	In March, Mugabe threatens to dissolve parliament and hold new elections.

FURTHER READING/INTERNET RESOURCES

Barclay, Philip. *Zimbabwe: Years of Hope and Despair*. New York: Bloomsbury USA, 2010.

Chikuhwa, Jacob W. *Zimbabwe: The Rise to Nationhood*. London: Minerva Press, 1998.

Owomoyela, Oyekan. *Cultures and Customs of Zimbabwe*. Westport, Conn.: Greenwood Press, 2002.

Rogers, Douglas. *The Last Resort: A Memoir of Zimbabwe*. New York: Crown, 2009.

Thorpe, Yvonne. *Zimbabwe (Global Hotspots)*. Salt Lake City: Benchmark Books, 2010.

Travel Information

http://travel.state.gov/travel/cis_pa_tw/cis/cis_1063.html
http://www.lonelyplanet.com/zimbabwe
http://www.tripadvisor.com/Tourism-g293759-Zimbabwe-Vacations.html

History and Geography

http://www.infoplease.com/ipa/A0108169.html
http://www.factmonster.com/ipka/A0108169.html
http://en.wikipedia.org/wiki/History_of_Zimbabwe

Economic and Political Information

https://www.cia.gov/library/publications/the-world-factbook/geos/zi.html
http://news.bbc.co.uk/2/hi/africa/country_profiles/1064589.stm
http://www.zimbabwesituation.com

Culture and Festivals

http://www.culturecrossing.net/basics_business_student.php?id=232
http://www.everyculture.com/Africa-Middle-East/Shona-Religion-and-Expressive-Culture.html
http://www.everyculture.com/To-Z/Zimbabwe.html

U.S. Embassy
172 Herbert Chitepo Avenue
Harare, Zimbabwe
(mailing address: P. O. Box 3340, Harare)
Tel: (+263) 4-250593/4
Fax: (+263) 4-722618
E-mail: consularharare@state.gov
Internet: http://harare.usembassy.gov

Zimbabwe Tourism Authority
Harare - Head Office
P.O. Box CY286, Causeway
Harare, Zimbabwe
Tel: (+263) 4-752570 or (+263) 4-758730/4
Fax: (+263) 4-758826/8
E-mail: webmaster@ztazim.co.zw
Internet: http://www.zimbabwetourism.co.zw

U.S. Department of State
Bureau of Consular Affairs
2201 C Street NW
Washington, DC 20520
Tel: (202) 736-9130
Internet: http://www.state.gov/

Publisher's Note: The websites listed on these pages were active at the time of publication. The publisher is not responsible for websites that have changed their address or discontinued operation since the date of publication. The publisher reviews and updates the websites each time the book is reprinted.

INDEX

Numbers in **bold italic** refer to captions.

CONTRIBUTORS/PICTURE CREDITS

Professor Robert I. Rotberg is Director of the Program on Intrastate Conflict and Conflict Resolution at the Kennedy School, Harvard University, and President of the World Peace Foundation. He is the author of a number of books and articles on Africa, including *A Political History of Tropical Africa* and *Ending Autocracy, Enabling Democracy: The Tribulations of Southern Africa*.

Michael Gray Baughan is a freelance writer living in Richmond, VA. He is the author of numerous research and study guides as well as a biography of Charles Bukowski. When he isn't stuck in front of the computer, Michael spends as much time as possible with his wonderful wife, Lizzie, and his twin girls, Callie and Ella.